The Body Decorated

Victoria Ebin

THAMES AND HUDSON

© Blacker Calmann Cooper Ltd, 1979
This book was designed and produced by
Blacker Calmann Cooper Ltd, London

Filmset by Southern Positives and Negatives (SPAN), Lingfield,
Surrey

Printed in Spain by Heraclio Fournier, S.A.

Library of Congress Catalog card number: 79-63812

Contents

Introduction

The body is the physical link between ourselves, our souls, and the outside world. It is the medium through which we most directly project ourselves in social life; our use and presentation of it say precise things about the society in which we live, the degree of our integration within that society, and the controls which society exerts over the inner man.

The eccentric or misanthrope, the 'drop-out' of our own times, demonstrates his rejection of conventional values by his physical appearance — an act sometimes perceived by others as aggressive and therefore likely to elicit hostility. We have sensitively attuned notions of how we think we should look, and while we are able to exercise free choice within a general context, the boundaries of that choice are sufficiently well defined to alert us to warning tremors when we step beyond them.

These conventions say cogent things about the values of any given society — urban as well as tribal. They provide the key to our perceptions of other people, and form the basis of our behaviour towards them. Nowhere is this fact more evident than in the accounts of the first voyages of the European explorers, filled as they are with physical descriptions of the men and women they encountered. This is how Captain Cook describes the people of Tahiti, in a journal dated July 1769: 'Both sexes paint their bodies *Tattow*, as it is called in their language, this is done by inlaying the Colour of black under their skins in such a manner as to be indelible. Some have ill design'd figures of men birds or dogs, the women generaly have this figure Z simply on ever[y] joint of their fingers and toes . . . they sometimes wear Turbands but their chief head dress is what they call *Tamou* which is human hair platted scarce thicker than common threed; of this I can safely affirm that I have seen peices near a Mile in length work'd upon one end without a knott, these are made and wore only by the women, five or six such pieces of which they will some times wind round their headd the effect of which if done with taist is very becoming. They have earrings by way of orniment but wear them only at one ear, these are made of Shells, Stones, berries, red pease and some small pearls which they wear three tied together but our Beeds, Buttons, &c very soon supply'd their places.' (*The Voyage of the Endeavour*, ed. J. C. Beaglehole).

Later accounts of tribal peoples tend to come from colonial officers and missionaries. Often they give detailed descriptions of the material objects used as accessories and adornment — the shape of bangles and the number of the beads. There are curious accounts of surgical operations, circumcision rites and scarring techniques and procedures such as knocking out the teeth. At the

1. In the highlands of New Guinea political units are small and are dominated by 'self-made' chiefs such as this one. At feasts these compete with each other in displays of wealth, both by wearing shell-decoration and by overwhelming each other with gifts of pigs and shell artifacts. They also paint their faces with charcoal and dark colours to make themselves appear fierce and to disguise their identity.

same time as they recorded such practices these foreign intruders were busily trying to extinguish them. Nearly everywhere they went they attempted to impose their own conceptions of the physical body on the people they encountered. They discovered that to prohibit the 'natives' from carrying out their ritual practices, such as body decoration, was a necessary step in demolishing the structure of their traditional beliefs. The missionary who quoted Holy Scripture to the effect that man is created in God's image and cannot therefore meddle with this divine gift, or the government

2. An Aiome man of New Guinea, with ear-puffs of wallaby fur; he has fixed a number of sticks in his nose which fan out of a hole specially incised in his septum.

Haida
Nootka
Kwakiutl
Salish
Hidatsa
Sioux
Timucua
Aztecs
Panare
Barasana
Kayapo
Txicão
Suia
Caduveo
MARQUESAS
ISLANDS

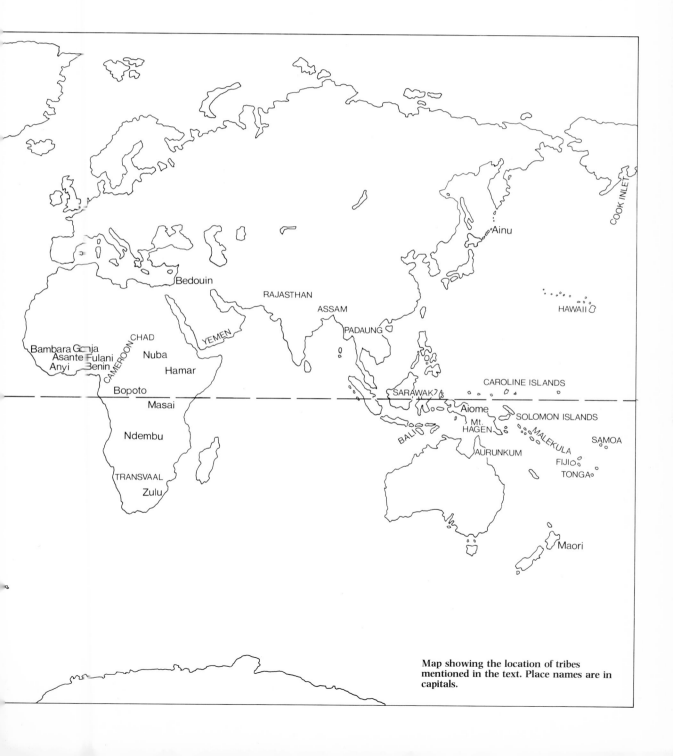

COOK INLET

Ainu

Bedouin

RAJASTHAN

ASSAM

PADAUNG

HAWAII

Bambara Gonja
Asante Fulani
Anyi Benin
CHAD
CAMEROON
Nuba
Hamar
YEMEN

Bopoto
Masai
CAROLINE ISLANDS

SARAWAK
Aiome
SOLOMON ISLANDS
Mt.
HAGEN
SAMOA

Ndembu
BALI
MALEKULA
FIJI
TONGA
AURUNKUM

TRANSVAAL
Zulu

Maori

**Map showing the location of tribes
mentioned in the text. Place names are in
capitals.**

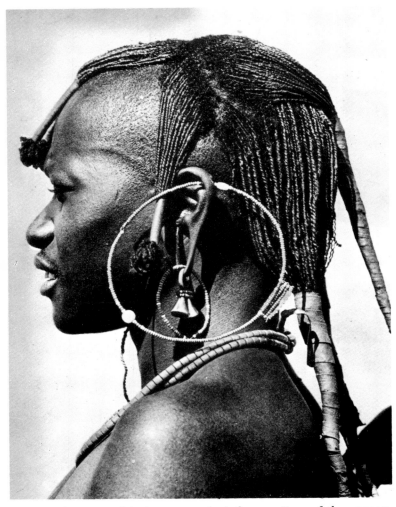

3. The hair of this Masai youth, which has been allowed to grow, has been rolled into long coils and then bound into sections. The ear lobes of these people often become greatly distended from the weight of their ear-rings; sometimes several ornaments are placed in a single hole. In wearing ornaments of this sort, the Masai are pursuing an ideal of beauty which was understandably in conflict with that of early missionaries and explorers.

official who reacted in horror against the practices of the savage, seemed both to be responding to the same threat — a xenophobic reaction which was expressed in daily encounters and in government policies.

Melville expressed a similar sense of alienation, a similar recoil from the unfamiliar. A famous passage in *Moby Dick* describes Queequeg, a 'counterpane of patchwork', carving the lid for his own coffin, striving to reproduce on it the twisted tattoos etched on his dying body: 'And this tattooing had been the work of a departed prophet and seer of his island, who by those hieroglyphic marks, had written out on his body a complete theory of the heavens and the earth, and a mystical treatise on the art of attaining truth; so that Queequeg in his own proper person was a riddle to unfold; a wondrous work in one volume; but whose mysteries not even himself could read, though his own live heart beat against them; and these mysteries were therefore destined in the end to moulder away with the living parchment whereon they were inscribed, and so be unsolved to the last. And this thought it

4. This New Guinean has inserted the horn of a scarab beetle in his nose to make himself look fierce.

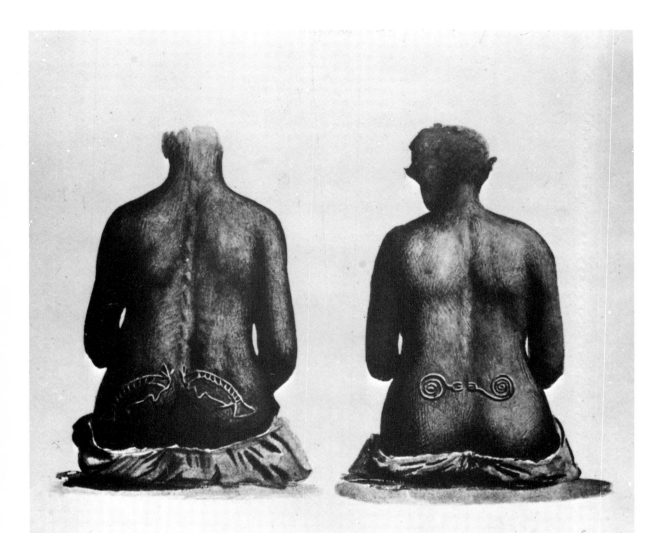

must have been which suggested to Ahab that wild exclamation of his, when one morning turning away from surveying poor Queequeg – "Oh, devilish tantalization of the gods!" '

It is not necessary to indulge in Melville's highly tinted mysticism to regard Queequeg's tattoos as amounting to a statement made by the individual about himself and his society. Such marks conform to Edmund Leach's definition of ritual behaviour as part of a signalling system, communicating information 'not because of any mechanical link between means and ends, but because of the existence of a culturally defined communication code.'

5. Artist's conception of designs scarred on the backs of two Polynesian women; note the striking resemblance of the one on the right to the famous photograph by Man Ray of a woman whose back has been transformed into a violin

6. The tattoos of this Sandwich Islands chieftain indicate his high status.

Dess. par S.Leroy d'après S.Arago. Gravé par Lerouge et Forget.

ÎLES SANDWICH. UN OFFICIER DU ROI EN GRAND COSTUME.

7 and 8. These illustrations show two types of neck chokers:
the one on the left is worn by a Chin woman from Padaung,
Burma. Her choker is built up from rings of rattan, each of
them enclosed in beaten brass. The illustration on the right
shows the thick beaded choker worn by a young Bakoba
bride from Transvaal. Trade goods such as brass or beads
were often used in decoration as a means of displaying
wealth. The rings would have been added slowly so that the
effect could be achieved without extravagant pain.

9. *(Left)* This youth is a member of the Wai-Wai, a Carib group living on the borders of Brazil and Guyana. His pride in the macaw feathers in his nostrils is evident.

10. *(Left)* Lip-plugs collected on George Vancouver's voyages around the Northwest coast of America (1790-95). The cased plug, about 5 inches long, is made of white quartz; it comes from Cook's Inlet, Alaska, and was obviously highly valued, since both the broken tips have been mended with sinew. The other two plugs are made of coiled cedar bark and wood; they would have been worn by Haida women of high rank.

11. *(Right)* Vast, wooden lip-plugs are worn by men as well as women in Chad; in other parts of West Africa they are made of stone, clay and quartz. Initially small cuts would be made, in this case in the upper lip. As the wound healed, larger and larger lip-plugs would be inserted. The increasing size of the plug would give added status to the wearer.

12. *(Left)* The Hamar of southern Ethiopia believe they can ensure physical and spiritual well-being by smearing their bodies with the entrails of a cow.

13. *(Right)* Fulani women of Niger paint their faces to ward off evil spirits and illness.

Elsewhere, Leach emphasizes that a vital element in ritual activity is the desire to gain mystical power. He defines such behaviour as 'potent in itself in terms of the cultural conventions of the actors, but not potent in a rational — technical sense. [It] is directed towards evoking the potency of occult powers even though it is not presumed to be potent in itself.' Body decoration equips man with the armament necessary to invoke the magic powers which he believes to be inherent in the natural world (plates 12, 13, 14, 15). He adorns himself with feathers in the hope that he will be as successful in his quest for wealth as the eagle in his predatory forages; in the same way he hopes to obtain the swiftness of a panther or the grace of an antelope. By painting his body with the spots of a leopard and by donning feathers from the Bird of Paradise he endows himself with the powers of those creatures, extending his own powers beyond the world he lives in and stepping beyond the limits of his own identity.

14. A Ghanaian priestess with facial designs painted in white clay. White represents the sacred nature of the gods, while the parallel lines across her forehead, representing the arc of the rainbow, are said to deflect the attacks of evil mystical beings.

15. *(Left)* This Ivory Coast shaman has painted her eyes with white clay, mixed with herbs and water from a sacred river so that she can see into the spirit world.

16. *(Right)* Woman from the Sandwich Islands, painted during J. Arago's voyage around the world, 1817-20.

17. *(Below)* Illustration from Duperrey's *Voyage de la Coquille* (1822-25); the artist has used considerable licence in his portrayal of the hair-styles, but has succeeded in conveying their considerable ornamental value.

18. *(Left)* Sioux Indian chief, decorated with war paint. On his chest are representations of the sun and moon which may be connected with the Sun Dance, an important event in the Sioux calendar. The drawing is from the *Codex Canadiensis* of around 1700. While we know a good deal about how the Sioux decorated themselves in the nineteenth century to indicate achievements in war, this is one of the first depictions of the Indians of the plains with such decoration.

This book examines body decoration in terms of these beliefs and their application to widely differing cultures. Chapter 1 shows how man demonstrates his identity as a member of a society by permanent forms of decoration – usually scarring, tattooing or deformation of the body. Adornment as a means to mark social status and to denote various forms of achievement is discussed in the second chapter. Chapter 3 examines the use of the body, particularly in a ceremonial context, as a means to display wealth and to convey power; and the final chapter looks at some of the techniques of tattooing, perhaps the most dynamic and visually fascinating of all forms of bodily adornment. In so brief a compass it has proved possible to select no more than a few specific cases in order to illustrate these general points and to bring out the salient characteristics of the art. However, these cases have been chosen to represent a wide variation of locale and culture, and to depict many different sorts of society. So have the many illustrations, each of which should be examined in close conjunction with the text.

19. An early nineteenth-century painting of a Marquesas Islander. The European artist, H. Ainsworth, has imposed his own perceptions on the native design, making it resemble a French military uniform. Despite the imprecise depiction of the body decoration, the picture conveys an idea of power, one of the original intentions of the Marquesas Islanders in being so decorated.

The Mark of Cain

20. The long scars on this Cameroon woman's face identify her as a member of a particular ethnic group. The gold ring in her nose is a sign of beauty and wealth.

'There must have been a time when the old Hebrew knew all about this custom of tribal marks. By this custom only can we fully understand the story of Cain (*Genesis 14, 15*) who fears to be sent from his own territory lest he be slain by the first stranger he meets, but is protected by the tribal mark of those among whom he is to wander being put upon him.' (Frederick Starr)

The first and essential fact of body decoration is that it distinguishes man as a social being, distinct from animals of the forest and other humans outside his own particular group — for he regards both as equally alien. Through decorating his body in some permanent form the individual expressly conveys his allegiance to his own group, making a precise distinction between those in society and those beyond its confines: it is the crucial factor in his relations with the rest of the world, the distinction between beauty and the beast.

The Bafia people of Cameroon, for instance, say that without their scarifications they would be indistinguishable from pigs or chimpanzees. The Maori woman of New Zealand claims that if she neglected to tattoo her lips and gums she would resemble a dog with her white teeth and red mouth (plate 21). The Nuba of the

21. This nineteenth-century photograph of a Maori, the sister of a queen, illustrates a facial tattoo which can occasionally be seen today. The pattern is considered to be only an abbreviated version of an earlier design, by then already abandoned as a result of missionary influence.

Sudan perceive that the crucial difference between men and animals lies in men's ability to shave their heads and bodies and to make their skins smooth. This capacity distinguishes them from every other species: even language was once shared between men and monkeys.

In New Guinea the Roro people, who tattoo themselves extensively, describe the un-tattooed person as 'raw', comparing him to uncooked meat. Claude Lévi-Strauss draws a fascinating distinction between raw and cooked meat on the one hand, and fresh and rotten fruit on the other: the former is transformed by a cultural process, the latter by a natural one. The Roro see the tattooed man as 'cooked meat', transformed by a human process and thus given a social identity. Therein lies the distinction between a social being and a biological entity.

The parts of the physical body which are decorated emphasize the individual's involvement with the outside world. Terence Turner has shown that the Kayapo Indians of central Brazil discriminate between the parts of the body in terms of red and

22. *(Above)* The young African n this picture, taken about seventy years ago, displays three distinct sets of scars. The cuts on his face were made by slashing the skin with a sharp knife; these on his torso were caused by rubbing an irritant into the wounds, as were the ridges snaking down his arms.

23. The facial scars on this woman from northern Ghana, now visible as lightly etched lines, were incised at birth.

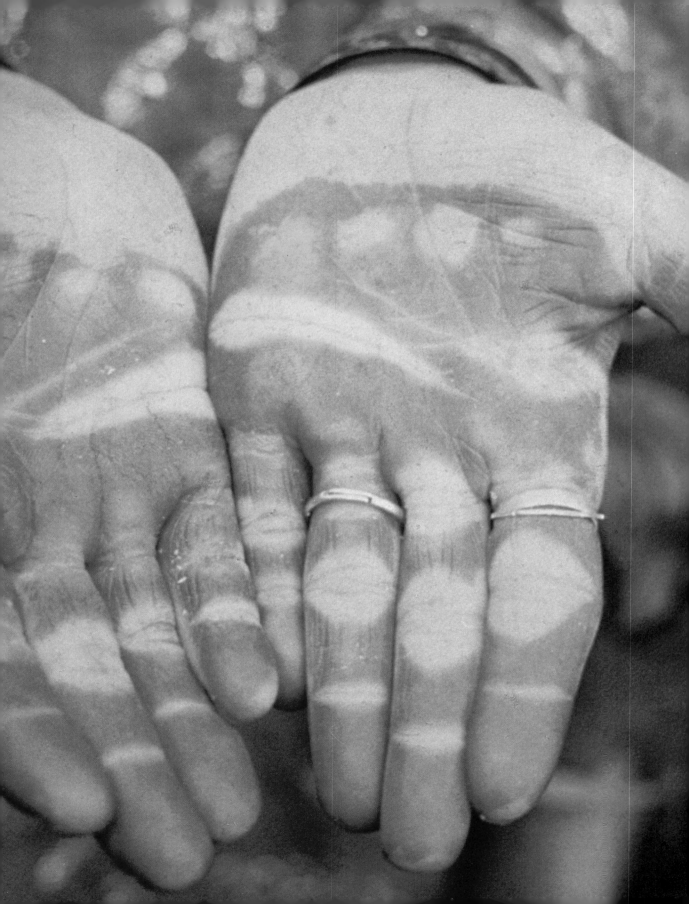

24-26. Decoration is commonly used to emphasize those parts of the body which are in frequent contact with the outside world. The Yemeni hand patterns shown here have been made by applying khidab. The foot design spreads over the toe-nails on to the sole; after it has been applied, the foot is bound in either cloth or a plastic bag to ensure that the skin sweats and that the paint lasts longer. These designs are used in cities in the Yemen and elsewhere in the Middle East by brides and their female relatives and friends at weddings. The designs take several weeks to wear off.

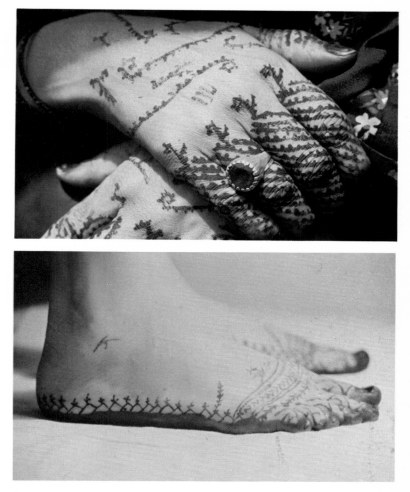

black. Red is associated with 'energy, health and "quickness", both in the sense of swiftness and heightened sensitivity'; it is applied on the parts of the body most immediately associated with swiftness, agility, and sensory contact with the outside world — the extremities and around the face. Black, the colour associated with transition states between clearly defined zones, is applied to the torso, signifying the integration of the inner man into social life.

The most frequently decorated parts are the hands, the feet and the mouth — i.e. our outward means of communicating with the outside world and the concentration points of our nerves and sensitivity. Examples of this theme are widespread: the Marquesa woman who must tattoo her hands or she cannot cook food, the Ainu woman who upon her marriage has her hands and mouth tattooed, the Maori woman who until recently insisted on tattooing her mouth (plate 21). Women in Arab countries dye their hands and feet with henna and frequently tattoo delicate patterns around their mouths (plates 24–26).

Many peoples make permanent marks upon the body in order to express enduring characteristics, such as clan affiliation

27. *(Left)* **An unusual form of scarification practised in southern Australia results in long coils of raised skin across the chest.**

(plate 28). They even radically change the shape of their bodies, moulding or modifying it to accord with aesthetic values which all members of their society hold in common and pronounce as the definition of beauty: not to be so marked excludes a person from social life (plates 36, 37, 38). In Bali, for instance, acceptance as a full member of society requires the filing of the teeth: pointed teeth are associated with monsters and non-human creatures, and

28. **Two youths, members of the same aboriginal group as the man shown in plate 27, display almost identical scars.**

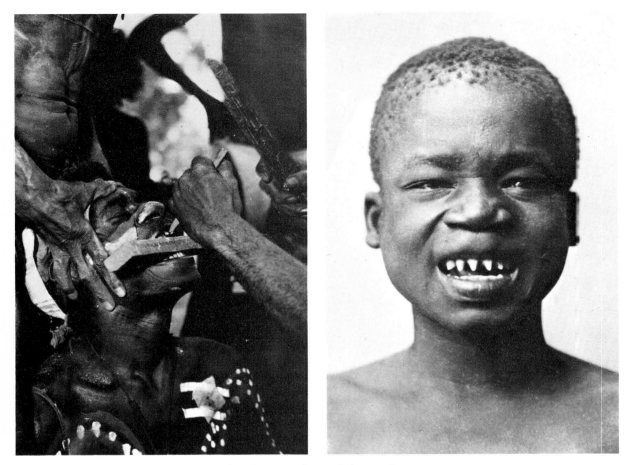

if a person dies before the operation has been performed the teeth of the corpse are ceremonially filed (plate 31).

Similarly, the Aowins of south-west Ghana are recognized by a diagonal scar on the left cheek, made eight days after birth. They believe that at death the soul travels to the spirit world, eventually to be reborn; so there is always the fear that an infant soul may choose to return to its spirit home, and the new-born child is therefore kept inside a house for its first seven days on earth. On the eighth day the official 'outdooring' ceremony is held. The infant and mother are brought into the sunshine and the child is presented to the family and the community. Until then, no one can be certain that the child truly belongs to this world.

Only when this period of seclusion is over, and the infant is still seen to be healthy, is he given a name appropriate to his family and scarred on his left cheek. Were he to die before this ceremony he would not be mourned; there would be no funeral and no one, not even his mother and father, would observe the mourning customs — he would be described as 'not a real person', only a spirit not meant for this world. By virtue of this ceremony, however, the infant is marked irrevocably as a member of the group, and should he die the next day he will still be entitled to commemoration as an

29. (*Above left*) An Australian aborigine bites a piece of wood while an elder clasps his head. The wood is then struck sharply with a knife-handle, in order to knock out the initiate's teeth.

30. (*Above*) In many parts of the world, people file their teeth to sharp points, often to enhance their beauty. This boy, from central Africa, has just undergone the operation.

31. In Bali, by contrast, sharp teeth are associated with monsters and the teeth of the Balinese are filed flat as a sign of human identification. This wall plaque, made from coloured rice, forms part of a ritual offering at a tooth-filing ceremony.

32-35. This series of pictures, from Gonja in northern Ghana, shows stages in a scarring ceremony seven days after the birth of an infant. The mother is not allowed to be present, and in the first plate (top left), it is the father's sister who holds the baby.

Cuts for the scars are made by a local barber and are incised with a knife in groups of three. Long slashes are made on the upper arms, twelve cuts radiate from the navel, resembling the rays of the sun, and another series runs along both sides of the face. After the operation the infant is bathed in a large calabash, filled with an infusion of medicinal leaves and warm water.

This form of scarification has become more rare in recent years, largely as a result of disapproval by the former colonial government. Scarification is now mostly confined to the abdomen, where it can be concealed by clothing.

This operation is very similar to that performed by the Aowins.

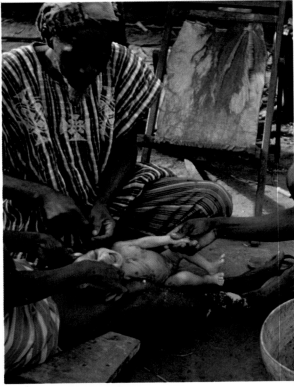

37. *(Above)* In Malekula in the New Hebrides it was once the practice to deform a boy's head by wrapping plaited leaves around it during infancy. Later, when he was about seven or eight years old, his ears were pierced with rings of turtle shell.

38. *(Right)* Bopoto mother and child: the infant's head has been bound with leaves to produce the elongation which these people admire.

36. *(Left)* A mid-nineteenth-century painting by Paul Kane of a Chinook Indian from the Northwest Coast of America: it shows the cradle and cedar-bark bundle with which parents flattened the shape of their infant's head to make it more beautiful.

ancestor. Here, as in many other societies, the mark which the child receives at birth both seals his identity and signifies his right to share in a common heritage. By acquiring a name he has acquired a permanent place among the Aowins and his social significance is writ upon his body (plates 32–35).

Among the American Indians of the Northwest Coast, a high-domed forehead was considered to be a feature of great beauty as well as a practical mark of distinction from neighbouring groups. These Indians, notably the Kwakiutl, the Salish and the Nootka, took practical measures to achieve such a look, and were designated as 'Flat-Heads' by early explorers. Shortly after her child's birth a mother would bind a board against its forehead at an angle which produced the sloping head peculiar to her own people; slight variations of the technique would result in different head shapes which served to distinguish one people from another at a glance (plate 36).

Within any one group of people, there are usually smaller groups based upon kinship or location. These allegiances form part of the structure of society, dictating marriage patterns, economic pursuits and certain privileges and prohibitions. The ornamentation of the body makes these distinctions immediately visible. A North

American Indian people, the Haida, were organized into lineages, each one taking as its totem an animal or natural phenomenon – a planet, a star or one of the winds. Members of a particular lineage, who could not marry those of another, and were subject to certain other prohibitions, were identifiable by the particular representation of their totem which they tattooed upon their arms and hands – a beaver, perhaps, or a wolf or an eagle.

An equally interesting example of body decoration as a means to maintain ethnic identity can still be seen among the Ainu people living on the island of Hokkaido in northern Japan. As a small group within a larger community which threatened to absorb them, the Ainu used once to practise a way of life which set them apart, dressing in their traditional clothes; although they lived in settlements of mixed population they were surrounded on all sides by the trappings of Japanese civilization. Their women could always be recognized by a wide blue tattoo on their upper lips. Like language and ritual practices, body decoration serves to set people apart from one another. It may be one of the last manifestations of their difference which they abandon and its demise usually signals the end of their special ethnicity.

Every group of people recognizes a particular set of symbols, adherence to which is implicit in the definition of their own society. The Bambara of West Africa, for instance, associate their origins with a mythical creature, half man and half beast, known as Chi Wara. Using his feet to claw the earth and his head and neck as a hoe, this creature tilled the soil, fertilizing it with a venom which he had inherited from his snake father, and through his efforts the crops grew. He taught men his technique, and after that they had plenty to eat; but eventually he saw that they wasted the food he gave them, and he departed from the earth.

Today the Bambara commemorate Chi Wara by marking their faces with eight small scars, two vertical ones under the nose and three under each eye, which they call *chi wara te*. This representation carries several connotations. It refers back to a common ancestor and emphasizes a common allegiance; it binds the Bambara together, expressing their unity against the outside world; and it stands for integrity and hard work, the values which have helped the tribe to survive in the face of misfortune and the indifference of the natural world – famine, drought and epidemics. During the harvest time men participate in hoeing contests and say that as they toil away to make the earth fruitful Chi Wara lives again. It is a powerful concept – a potent symbol of the society which is marked upon all its members, making men subject to its imprint; they are the carriers of its force, like burdened ants.

39. The highly colourful body-painting of this Amazonian Indian enables him to make a flamboyant statement about the initiating ceremony of the boy he is decorating.

Symbols of Status

40. These Australian aborigines have been painted for an initiation ceremony: their designs are not washed and are allowed to wear off gradually.

A prime function of the body is to identify the individual's status within society, portraying in visible terms the individual's progression from infancy through puberty to adulthood. The outward signs of physiological development are not enough: they need to be accompanied by ritual acts, marking the progress of time and the passage of the individual through the life cycle.

In Western societies the church and its ceremonies mark these transitions in the individual's life – baptism, confirmation, marriage, death – while the passage of time, from season to season, is marked by religious festivals. Tribal societies mark them by ritual ceremonies, often reflecting the age groups around which many of them are structured (plates 41, 42, 43). Distinctions between these groups are strictly defined in terms of rights and duties, and they are often precisely indicated by appearance. Membership is central to the round of the male's daily activities and to the

41. Young boys from New Britain in full body-painting. At the time when this photograph was taken, the aborigines had no way of knowing what they looked like; the design worn by each individual was applied by someone else who used the body of a third person as a model.

selection of his friends; throughout his life he will retain ties with the companions of his youth, those with whom he played as a small boy serving with him when he has become a member of the political core of village life and one of the respected elders of the community. Such groups seem to be more important for men than for women since male activities are based on collective enterprises – hunting, politics and warfare. Similar effects persist in Western society – hence the continued existence of men's colleges, clubs and other social organizations which debar women from participation in the outside world.

For both males and females the onset of puberty is a dramatic event and is marked by ritual. Merely to reach physiological maturity does not qualify the adolescent for the rights and privileges due to the adult. To be officially accepted as such he must pass through a ceremony of which one significant element is the visible marking of the transition upon his body. While a boy or

42. Two Masai youths display the scars and hair style appropriate to their age group: note the use of safety pins.

43. Panare boys of southern Venezuela are initiated between the ages of eight and twelve. In this picture, the elders are holding objects which the boys will wear as a mark of their new status – beads for armbands, toucan pelts, necklaces made from the canine teeth of monkeys and loin-cloths which have been freshly painted with traditional geometric shapes. The ropes tied around their legs are made from their own and their wives' hair.

girl may be sexually mature, each is prohibited from sexual activity until the appropriate ritual has been performed (plates 44, 45). Circumcision may be carried out on the young male, clitoridectomy may be performed on the girl; in either case, as the old identity is left behind, the body itself is permanently transformed.

Rites of transition can be seen in terms of three stages, known to anthropologists as *separation*, *marginality* (an ambiguous period when the usual rules of society do not prevail) and *aggregation*. The initiate must first be removed from his former way of life; alone or with others of his status, he is led away from the community, and for a lengthy period — sometimes of several months — he will live apart and undergo certain ritual ordeals. Even if he remains physically within the community, he is cut off from social relationships and denied any identification with everyday life; he has no claims or rights to status, and his isolation is represented as a sort of death (plate 46). Sometimes this isolation is signified

44 and 45. Female initiation rites are significant among the matrilineal people of southwestern Ghana. Shortly before her marriage, the girl is ceremonially bathed in a river and is instructed by an older woman of her own lineage in the knowledge that she will need as a wife and mother.

After the bath, which is said to purify the girl and make her ready for childbearing, butter made from shea nuts is smeared over her. Later, dressed in new cloth and laden with gold ornaments which belonged to her family, she parades through the town, to be admired by the young men.

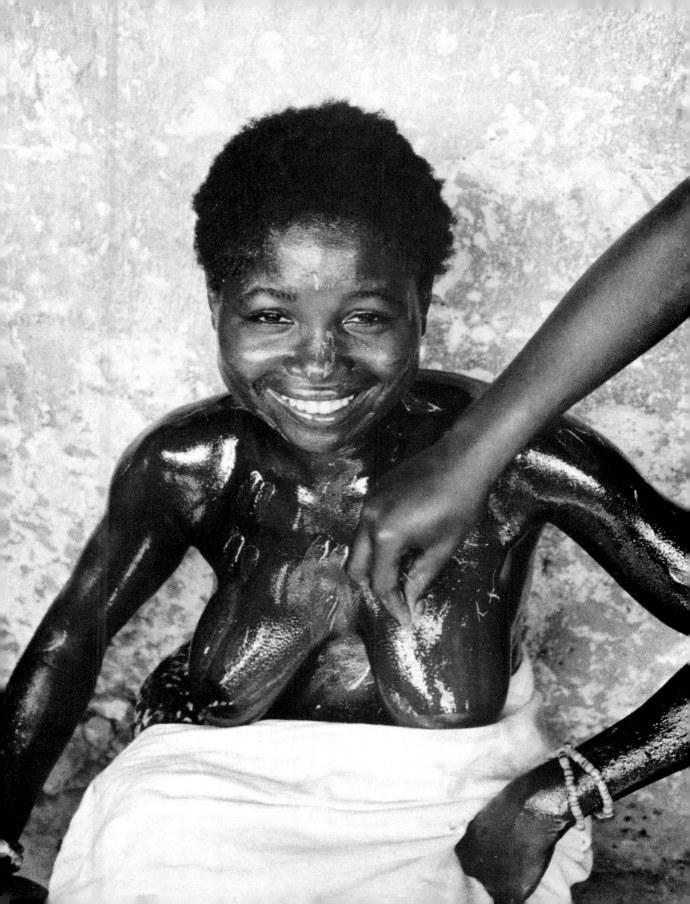

visually by the use of body adornment; initiates may coat their bodies with white clay – a material often associated with mourning. The place in which they are secluded may be referred to as a place of death: it is an unnatural time – the world is in a topsy-turvy state and the usual order and the expected pattern of events do not exist. Finally, having acquired the physical signs of their new status, the initiates are brought back into the community, ready for integration into adult society.

Most male initiation rites involve circumcision. Among the Bavole of northern Rhodesia a boy who has not been circumcised is not eligible to enter the social and political sphere of adult men. He is not entitled to their privileges, he cannot eat with the men or enjoy a sexually active life; in a state of permanent pollution, he is a pariah, avoided both by women who will not sleep with him and by other men to whom he represents a source of danger.

Circumcision is performed upon all the boys of a particular age group at the same ceremony. Among the Ndembu of Rhodesia it is a relatively uncomplicated operation. With a razor, one of the senior men of the community, known for his steady hand, slits around the prepuce which is then cut off, leaving the glans well exposed. It is no longer something shameful and dirty which must be covered. The pollution of the uncircumcised is said to arise because of the 'dark, unclean' condition of the penis which harbours bodily secretions. Medicinal balms used to heal the torn flesh have symbolic associations with the rites: one of them is described by the phrase 'it reveals the hidden'.

In addition to visible signs of manhood, initiates also need to acquire the specialized knowledge expected of all adult men. While their wounds heal the boys are instructed in hunting lore and the rules of behaviour which distinguish the adult from the adolescent. They are told not to laugh at the aged, not to swear and to get along well with their peers. The adult man, they are told, is courageous: after facing the circumcisor's razor, what have they left to fear?

At the end of the boy's seclusion, a series of small scars is made upon his face and abdomen which is said 'to give him back his body again'. The period of transition is at an end; after the ambiguity of being neither one thing nor another, of existing in a limbo, he has at last acquired his new status. The boys' arrival back to town is a festive occasion; the women have brewed quantities of beer to greet them, and they pretend not to recognize their sons in their transformed state.

As the transition is marked upon the body, the inner man too cannot escape being deeply scarred. The mark he bears is not only

46. Male initiation rites among the Australian aborigines are deliberately terrifying; in this case they are accompanied by chanting and the rhythmic beating of sticks.

on the surface; the rites nearly always involve excruciating pain, giving potent force to the notion that the individual dies and is re-born in a new identity.

In the Tanga islands of Melanesia there exists a secret society, the Sokapana, the members of which possess the special status of those who have encountered death and have been born again. Greatly feared by the rest of the community, they are recognized by long symmetrical scars cut deeply into their backs — scars that are reckoned to be proof of their claim to have met with the dead and to have been incised by the teeth of the ghosts who swallowed them before they were reborn.

To become a member of the Sokapana, the initiate must face terrifying ordeals. On the day of his initiation the senior members of the society meet at a house in the forest, making a fearsome din with bullroarers and pipes to announce to the villagers that the ghosts have arrived. Within the house the men prepare to welcome the initiates by decorating themselves with grotesque and frightening costumes: some wear masks which represent a dangerous species

47. *(Above left)* **Bopoto woman of central Africa: the raised scars were made at different times to signify the stages of her development. They were caused by slashing the skin and rubbing ash into the wound.**

48. *(Above right)* **To conform with the practices of their age group, these young Nuba men have carefully shaved their hair and have whitened one side of their faces.**

of fish, others dress as warriors, clenching false beards in their mouths and smearing their bodies with red and yellow paint. The hapless initiate is led to the door of the house, whereupon he is surrounded by these masked and intimidating figures and becomes the centre of a fierce battle in which he symbolically dies. Occasionally, men are indeed killed during the skirmish and their families must be satisfied with the explanation that he was killed by one of the ghosts. Then, while the initiate is in a symbolically dead state, he receives the scars upon his body which from now on will distinguish him as one who has confronted the ghosts and survived the ordeal.

The Sokapana initiate must also pass through a series of other trials. The head of the society whips him with a thin brown cane across the calves, thighs and back, and the weals thus raised are outlined in a layer of soot. A kinsman of the initiate makes a series of cuts on his calves, about three-quarters of an inch long and about half an inch apart, by raising up a small piece of skin and slicing it with a sharp knife. More scars are made upon his back with a hooked thorn, known as the 'teeth of the ghost', with which the skin is hooked up and cut. To show any sign of pain during the operation, to scream or cry out, will bring the anger of the ghosts and the initiate may be killed. Afterwards, other members of the society jump up to receive a whipping of their own and additional scars to mark their seniority.

For about a month after the scars have been made the initiate is not allowed to speak. He covers himself with soot and dresses himself as if he were in mourning, claiming afterwards that he was swallowed up by a ghost which vomited him forth, leaving the raised scars on his back. He has died and been reborn after an encounter with the terrifying creatures of the underworld.

Another of the various bodily signs of social status is achieved by means of the tattoo. This is performed at all stages of physical development but the most profuse and intricate designs are generally not applied until the youth is aged between fifteen and twenty, since the patterns would be distorted by continuing growth. A few small designs may be made during childhood, but these are generally confined to the face and are intended to protect the child from illness and spirits.

At least until the early years of this century, the Marquesas Islander had to be tattooed in order to become an active member of the community. A woman whose hand lacked a particular blue design was not allowed to knead the dough which formed the staple of the islanders' diet, and a man who had not been tattooed with the other youths of his age was exiled from community life.

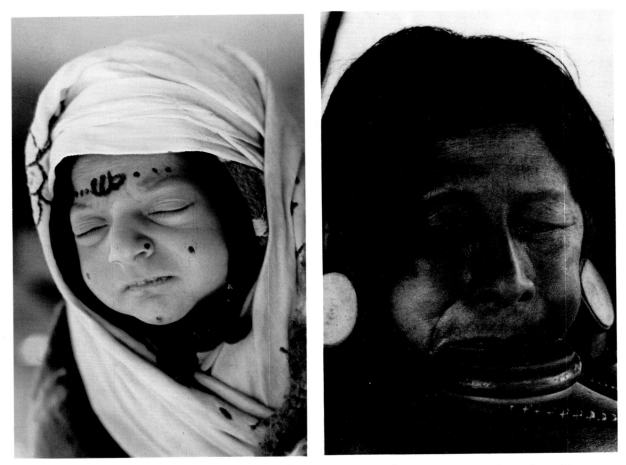

Girls received their first tattoo when they were between seven and twelve years old, while boys — whose tattooing covered the body more completely — went through a series of initiation rites between the ages of fifteen and twenty.

A father was expected to arrange for the tattooing of his first-born son, and those youths of the community who did not have this favoured position were allowed to make use of the service of the tattoo artist summoned for the occasion. The first-born had an advantage over the others, acquiring an elaborate suit of tattoo immediately while the rest received theirs piece-meal. While there seems to have been no difference in the design given to the first-born and to the others, there was a variation in the order in which tattooing was performed. The first-born was tattooed from the feet up, but the other boys received their first marks on the face. The body was not totally covered until old age, and the most complete decoration was reserved for the old and wealthy members of the community — for only they could afford the cost of summoning the tattoo artist and paying him and his assistants. The design would be renewed constantly throughout the individual's life, since it faded over the years, and amongst the old its delicacy might be obscured by being repeatedly gone over.

49. *(Above left)* **The marks on this Yemeni infant's face are made with khidab. The letters across his forehead spell out 'Allah' to protect him from evil spirits; his coverings carry similar designs.**

50. *(Above right)* **Suiá man of Brazil, wearing wooden discs on his ear-lobes and the plugs which distinguish adults from their juniors.**

ÎLES CAROLINES: ÉTUDE DE DEUX CAROLINOIS DANSANT.

51. This charming early nineteenth-century print, showing Caroline Islanders dancing – or perhaps wrestling – is typical of the romantic attitude to tribal societies which prevailed in Europe at the time it was made.

The ceremony for the first-born son was scheduled well in advance of the appointed time and the boy's father would have had to plant extra crops and to raise pigs in order to feed the other youths (sometimes as many as fifty) and to pay the tattoo artist for his services. A special house was built where the boys lived with the artist and his assistants, for they were all considered to be sacred during this period and therefore vulnerable. Contact with the outside world was dangerous, both to themselves and to other members of the community to whom they were a source of pollution. They could have nothing to do with women. On the morning on which the tattooing began the young men raided the homestead of the father, tearing down his house, stealing his pigs and foraging in his gardens; they then secluded themselves in the house with their loot and the tattoo artist set to work, starting with the first-born son, who was held down by the other youths, while his assistants fanned away the flies.

On completion of the tattooing the house was burned down and all who had participated in the rite went to bathe in the sea, covering themselves in fragrant oil to give the skin a yellow sheen against which the blue-black tattoo glistened brilliantly. A stage had been prepared in the centre of the town to which the first-born

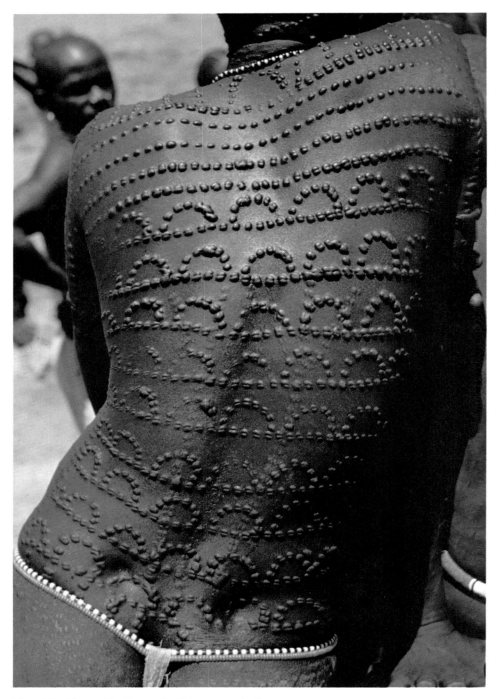

52 and 53. The scarification on the Nuba women in these two illustrations marks important events in their lives. The scars on the girl on the right would have been made at the onset of puberty. A further set have been added to the woman on the left after the weaning of her first child, in order to signify her return from the seclusion of childbirth. The scarification is achieved by hooking the skin with a thorn and then cutting it with a small knife, thus leaving a protruding scar. The scars are considered to enhance the woman's sexual appeal.

led the young men on a ceremonial parade. The young girls joined them there and prepared themselves to celebrate the beginning of the cutting ceremonies.

In most societies which permanently mark their bodies a woman's marriage or the birth of her first child requires a further significant transformation in her physical appearance (plates 52, 53). The Ainu of Japan, for instance, distinguish the married woman from the unmarried by the blue moustache tattooed on her lips, a small version of which was made at puberty; it now acquires its final full-blown shape, spreading nearly from ear to ear. The woman's hands are tattooed at the same time, the two sets of marks signifying that her loyalties and duties are from now on attached solely to her husband: she is bound to him in all that she utters and her hands will labour only to prepare his food and work on his behalf.

The women make the tattoos upon each other, the older ones capturing the young girl and holding her down as another woman slashes her upper lip. Pigment is rubbed into the wound to create the fanciful upturned wings of the moustache. In former times, according to modern accounts of older women, a young girl who re-used this operation could not expect to attract a husband. However, as Ainu women began to marry with the Japanese population of the island, the practice began to die out. Today, many women say they are thankful that they can avoid the painful operation, asserting that in daily life they do not miss a mark which sets them so dramatically apart from the Japanese. Nonetheless, there are still occasions when young Ainu women claim that they

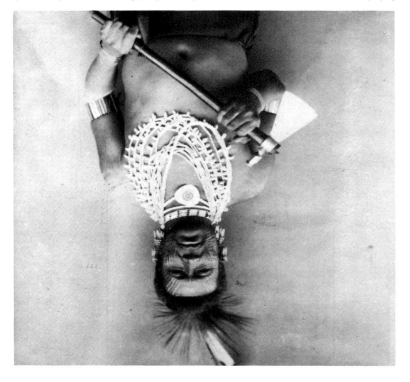

54. (*Left*) Eagle feathers were widely used both on their own and in headdresses to signify important events in the lives of warriors of the North American Plains Indians. This photograph was taken by Prince Roland Bonaparte, a famous photographer of tribal peoples who first visited America in 1888.

55. (*Right*) Scarification forms an important part of Bopoto initiation rites. Here, cuts are made with a razor and blood is prevented from dripping on the ground for fear of offending the gods.

56. (*Right*) A sixteenth-century water-colour by John White of an Eastern Timucua Indian from northeast Florida. The body designs are probably tattoos. This practice was confined to chiefs and their wives, indicating the wearer's high status, as this practice was confined to chiefs and their wives. His face is painted red, in preparation for war.

57. (*Overleaf*) Australian aborigines from Aurunkun, Cape York Peninsula, painting themselves in preparation for clan dances, in which they re-enact stories from their mythological past.

wish to join their elders, dressed in the traditional dress and marked with the traditional sign of their married status. On one especially festive occasion within the recent past, some of the younger women imitated the moustache with a blue pen: the elder women, not deceived for a moment, drove them from their circle and resumed their stately promenade.

Membership in an age group often carries the right to certain specific forms of ornamentation denied to others. Among the Nuba of the Sudan, for instance, the youngest males are recognizable by their use of red ochre and their simple hair-styles, while the oldest are entitled to a more flamboyant range of colours and more elaborate hair-styles. Senior members are allowed to use rich black — a colour esteemed by those involved in dangerous activities because it is said to protect them from the evil eye of their enemies and because it can be smoothed over the body to make the wearer appear larger to his adversary. Upon reaching the most advanced of all the age groups, when they no longer take part in athletic pursuits, the Nuba cease to decorate their bodies. Instead, they cover themselves with clothes, abandoning their wax hair-styles and usually keeping their heads shaved: their bodies are no longer exposed because they are no longer attractive.

Age is not, of course, the sole criterion by which status is judged among tribal societies. Another is achievement, either of an athletic or of a military nature, and this too is frequently expressed by means of a complex code of body decoration. In societies where no great distinctions exist between standards of living — where every-body eats essentially the same food, houses are built of the same

sorts of material, and dress is dictated by common considerations of climate and availability – physical adornment is one of the few means by which the individual can express either his status or his prowess.

A warrior of the Hidatsa, an Indian tribe of North America, signified his military exploits by decorating himself with feathers according to a closely defined code (plate 54). The number of men he had killed could be calculated precisely from his appearance: a red feather with a few strands of horse hair attached to it signified that he had killed an enemy, a feather with one red bar signified that he was the second person to strike, and further bars indicated the strikers of succeeding blows. If he had been wounded in battle, he was entitled to wear a red feather; if he had killed a woman he wore a feather with a bound quill. One nineteenth-century traveller among the Hidatsa noted such practices. A spot on the larger section of the feather denoted an enemy killed; a feather coloured red on the top and with a notch removed signified that the wearer had cut the enemy's throat and taken his scalp; a feather clipped on the top, removing its natural point, meant that the wearer had cut the throat of an enemy; and a feather split along the quill denoted that the wearer had been wounded many times by the enemy.

58. The body of this Tuba girl has been oiled in preparation for a dance. Her scars date from the onset of puberty.

Ceremonial Decoration

59. In Mount Hagen, New Guinea, the colour red has symbolical associations for women, who wear it for the sake of its brightness and for its connotations of fertility; men wear it in order to make themselves look attractive.

60 and 61. Sabra, off the coast of New Guinea; two widows are painted in preparation for the ritual of mourning their husbands.

The most elaborate forms of decoration are generally seen on ceremonial and ritual occasions, involving lengthy preparation and much expense. Just as the appearance of the individual participant is intrinsic to the rite and to its performance, so the adornments worn are vital to the ritual theme (plates 60, 61). During one initiation rite in northern Ghana, for example, the men paint themselves with white clay, drawing a lattice of stripes across their bodies so that they strikingly resemble skeletons: they are deliberately draw-

62. (Overleaf) Among the Barasana of the Vaupés region of Colombia, men and women paint themselves in preparation for the dances which accompany the ceremonial exchange of food between groups. This man paints a careful design in red on his face, onto which he has first rubbed red pepper in order to make the paint adhere better.

ing death and destruction into their world, pervading their usual social space with a potent reminder of the surrounding disorder and the imminent threat.

Andrew and Marilyn Strathern have shown how Mount Hageners in New Guinea use body decoration to make statements about the nature of a particular occasion. In time of war, for example, their body painting, their facial designs and the accessories which they display all transmit the same distinct message of fierceness and aggressive power; their bodies are charcoaled to a deep black hue (also associated with poison) and among the ornaments they wear is one shaped like the wings of a particular bird whose presence is seen as an evil omen; they abandon glossy leaves, which symbolize health and well-being, in favour of the flat grey ones which they wear on days of mourning. The men display as a group: gathered together as one huge and overwhelming force, their individual identities are obscured under their decorations. Together, they represent the dark collective anger of the community, past and present.

At other celebrations the same men wear gleaming aprons made of pigs' tails plaited together and patterned with red ochre; the dancers' legs and their weapons are both painted with white wavy lines, perhaps intended to represent the patterns of light reflected in water, and they place red and white feathers in the hair, painting their faces in the same two colours. All of these decorations emphasize 'brightness' — an admired quality which is especially associated with two colours, red and white, and with certain objects such as feathers and shiny leaves (plate 59). Because the brilliant red flowers of the kilt tree are known to attract birds the men wear head-dresses made from the resin of that tree, adding red ochre and pronouncing ritual incantations to increase their brilliance. They also adorn themselves with big shells, for these too are regarded as 'bright' (plate 67).

63-67. The people of Mount Hagen in New Guinea share in an elaborate network of exchange relationships between neighbouring groups, competing with each other in the size and value of their gifts. These relationships are expressed on ceremonial occasions (*moka*) for which the men decorate themselves lavishly with feathers, shells and animal skins — objects which are both valuable in themselves and possess symbolic significance. The men in each group equip themselves with similar sorts of ornament distinguishing donors from recipients and denoting their wearers' importance. The decoration also signifies the different roles of the sexes: the men, who are in charge of preparations for war and exchange transactions, have more brilliant body decoration than the women whose duties are primarily domestic and agricultural.

63. Wigs form an essential part of the decoration. They are made of human hair, sometimes applied to a frame made of bark-cloth; burrs are attached to the frame, and hair is then stuck to the burrs. Here, a participant is fixing an eagle's feather in his head-dress. His red plumes are from a Bird of Paradise; he has placed ferns in his beard and he wears a cassowary bone in one ear.

65. Live pigs are given away during the course of a *moka*. Note the bamboo slats hanging down the men's chests; each represents a tally, signifying that in a single *moka* its wearer gave away between eight and ten shells.

66. Men are protected against contamination from menstrual blood by eating a ceremonial meal in a sacred enclosure barred to women. Here, they have just completed the meal, and are dancing out of the enclosure in pairs; some bear large shells, while others merely hold out their arms in imitation.

64. *(Left)* Returning to the enclosure, the men remove their feathers and decoration, and offer their visitors pieces of meat which they catch on the tips of their spears.

Such objects are used not only because the Mount Hageners like the things associated with them, money and wealth, but also because their very 'brightness' has the power to attract more of the same things by magic; they are seen as instrumental as well as expressive. Like praying or like uttering a spell the use of such a talisman, glowing with symbolic associations, has magical powers.

The display of the body makes statements about the individual, too. A man will use it both to accentuate his sexual attractiveness and his physical strength and to proclaim his wealth and status; in a sense he becomes greater than himself. The King of Benin, for instance, sits in state on festival occasions, an immoveable figure, almost unable to walk without assistance; around his ankles he wears heavy bands of metal, his face is nearly obscured by a head-dress and thick strings of coral are piled high around his neck from chest to chin. He remains seated through the festival while his subjects come to bow before him: it is as though they are paying homage to an idol, a symbol of the power of the state.

In stratified societies in particular, the body is the field upon which people demonstrate their personal holdings of wealth and status. Sexual appeal and the appearance of strength are obviously

67. Pearl shells used once to be exchanged for valuables from other regions, forming part of the bride price demanded of a man by his in-laws. They are esteemed for their gleaming surfaces, which are said to attract further wealth by magic. Before the influx of Australian currency, the shells were even more highly valued than they are today, and each was individually named.

68. *(Above)* A group of Australian aborigines about to set out on a hunting expedition; they have painted themselves with white clay as a protective measure. Note the similarity of their body patterns to that of the New Hollander painted by M. F. Peron (plate 70).

69. Elaborately plumed headdresses and vivid body painting are worn to celebrate the killing of a lion by the son of a Kenyan chief.

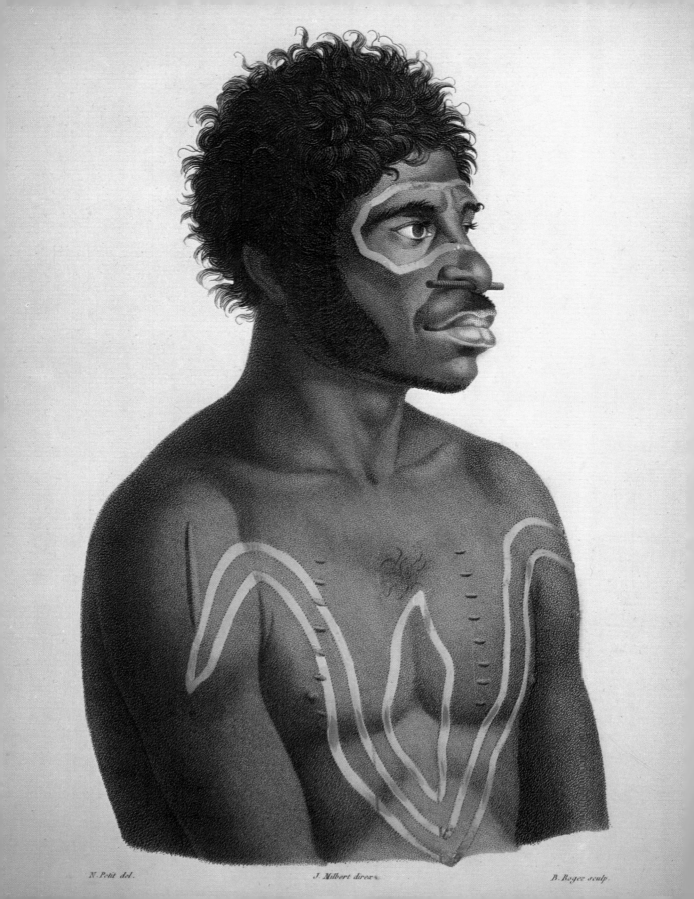

N. Petit del.   J. Milbert direx.   B. Roger sculp.

70. *(Left)* Portrait of a New Hollander, painted in 1802 by M. F. Peron.

71. This Asante woman, who has just given birth, has painted designs on her body with a mixture of leaves and white clay in order to provide mystical protection for herself and her infant.

73. *(Right)* Huge gold ear-rings represent the material wealth of this Fulani woman of Mali.

best achieved by enhancing what is there already, but the body can also serve as a display counter for valuables of a more material kind — objects from the owner's hoard of calculable wealth. Their added values are superimposed upon the self and in their social presentation the two are inextricably bound together (plates 73, 74).

Wedding ceremonies make this statement most clearly. In India, for example, marriage involves the transfer of property from one family to another, and the wedding ceremony crystallizes the terms of the exchange. The bride personifies this transference by her physical appearance when, adorned in the jewellery and precious stones which form her patrimony, she crosses over from her own family to that of the bridegroom; on that one day the power structure of society and the values which that society attaches to sex and property are both entwined upon her person. Her body provides the tally of the power relations which bind two families, it is the living medium which most vividly symbolizes the exchange between the contracting parties.

72. Two girls of the Solomon Islands: they have used root juices to paint their bodies for a ceremonial occasion.

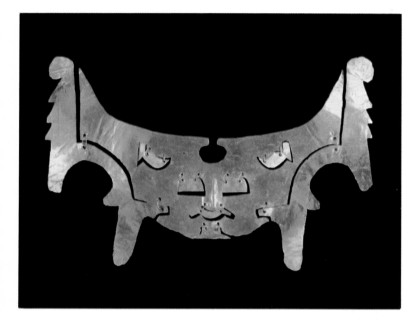

74. (*Left*) Beaten gold nose ornament from Calima, Colombia: it was made at least 700 years ago and was probably taken from a grave. It is 7 inches (17.5 cm) long.

77. (*Right*) Txicão Indians from the Xingu National Park, Brazil. Their body painting indicates the age groups to which they belong.

75. (*Below left*) A Barasana woman of Colombia decorates herself for a dance with red paint obtained from the sediment of specially boiled leaves. The black pigment with which she has outlined her forehead and temples is invisible when applied and only takes on colour as it oxidizes.

76. (*Below*) The Indians of the Xingu National Park in Brazil cut their hair in pudding-bowl fashion; they then coat their heads with red pigment made from urucu seeds and smoothed over the surface of the hair by means of string held tautly between the fingers. Sometimes another design, painted in black, is drawn upon the red cap.

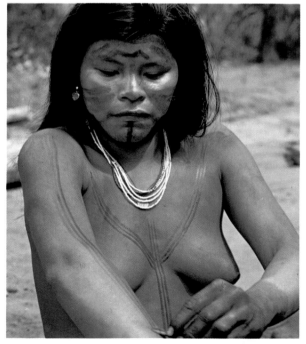

In our own society, too, this concentration most often devolves upon the woman: dressed in gold and precious stones she advertises her charms and adds to them, offering herself as a prize or toy, and representing in her person those two prime bases of power, sex and wealth. She is seen as the medium through which the struggle for power is acted out. In the socialist state, by contrast, or in egalitarian societies where labour and riches have already been allocated, power does not rest upon the attainment of such goods and the body has no part to play in such a ferocious barter arrangement.

In the aggressive society of Mount Hagen men struggle for dominance over one another, displaying their wealth and proclaiming their status by their physical appearance. 'Big men' gain in authority by accumulating valuables which they lend out to others for special occasions; power is expressed in terms of economic superiority. Similarly, the Eskimo tattoos across his forehead the flukes of the whales he has killed, the Trobriander wears shell armlets which he also uses for trading purposes, the Ekoi of Nigeria believe that the scars on their bodies will serve them as money on their journey to the place of the dead. Similarly, too, the Inca priest, at the peak of his hierarchical society, is adorned with gold.

Such material objects which may in themselves be worth no more than anything else our fancy may alight upon, often possess an additional value by virtue of their symbolic associations. Gold, for instance, is not only treasured for its price per ounce but also represents other values of which we approve. To the Aztecs it was associated with the sun; in Ghana it is valued on two grounds — because it comes from the earth, which gives it a mystical significance, and because of the Asante tradition that it can be found at the foot of the rainbow. In Western society, too, we deck ourselves out in costly objects which we also deem to be beautiful or symbolic: our aesthetic and our material values are synchronized. When we delight ourselves with objects which to us are beautiful but have little monetary value — earrings made of tiny shells, necklaces of pine cones — we are likely to provoke little more than the amusement of our friends: pretty, yes, but peculiar. If coupled with a particular label, however, such objects become respectable: when Saks Fifth Avenue sells lobster claw pendants with a high price tag we can indulge our tastes for marine bric-à-brac and still be taken seriously.

Such associations are by no means universal. As James Faris notes, the flamboyant body painting practised by the Nuba of the Sudan aims only to enhance the body, not to obscure it or to

78-81. The Hamar of southern Ethiopia, near Lake Turkana, construct elaborate coiffs *(boro)* when planting is finished or to celebrate a successful hunt. First the hair is trimmed, then clay is smoothed over the head from back to front.

78. A strand of hair is being plaited, prior to being coated with clay. Colour is then applied to the clay by flicking on red powder with a brush.

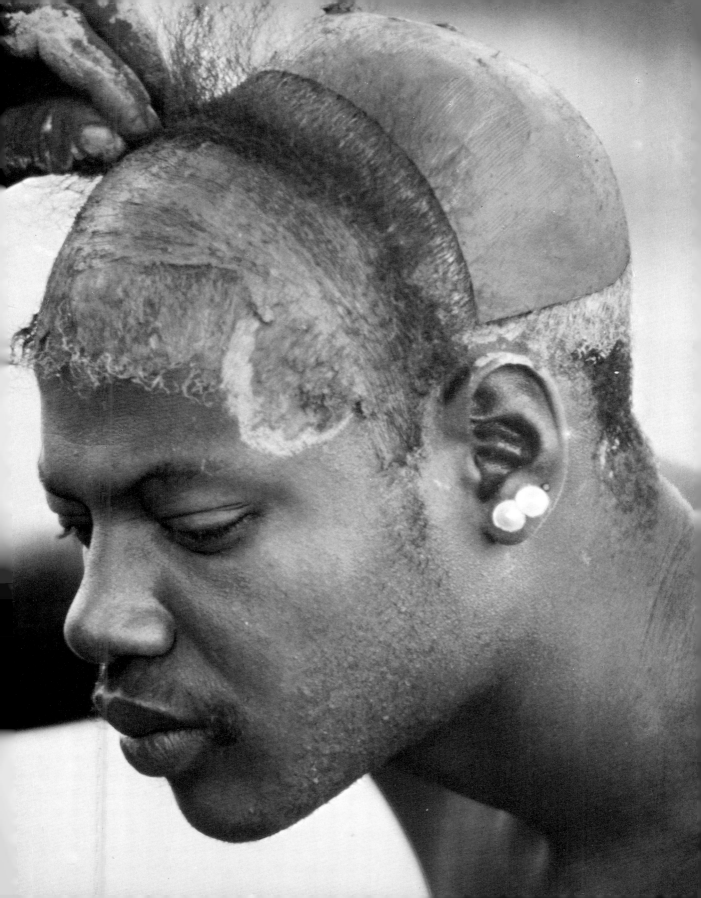

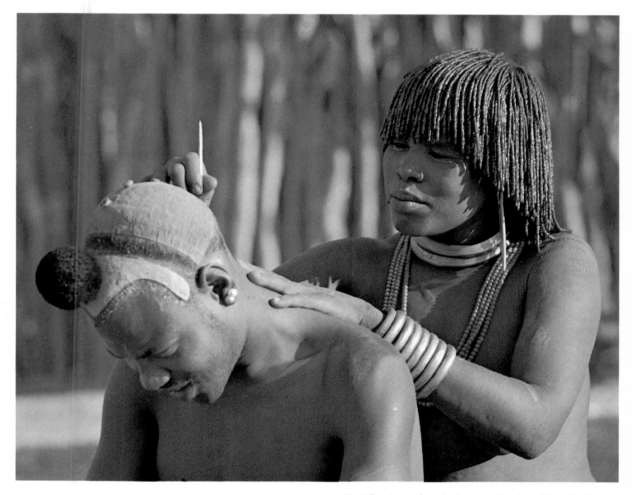

80. (*Above*) **A girl pricks holes in the clay of her friend's** *boro* **to prevent it from cracking when the hair grows beneath it. Her own coiffure is made by rolling strands of hair with ochre, butter and acacia gum.**

79. (*Left*) **The boy is admiring his reflection in a bowl of water.**

81. (*Overleaf*) **This plate shows the completed** *boro*. **The feathers are highly valued: the young men exchange them amongst themselves, and senior men of the tribe have the right to demand particularly fine specimens from the youths.**

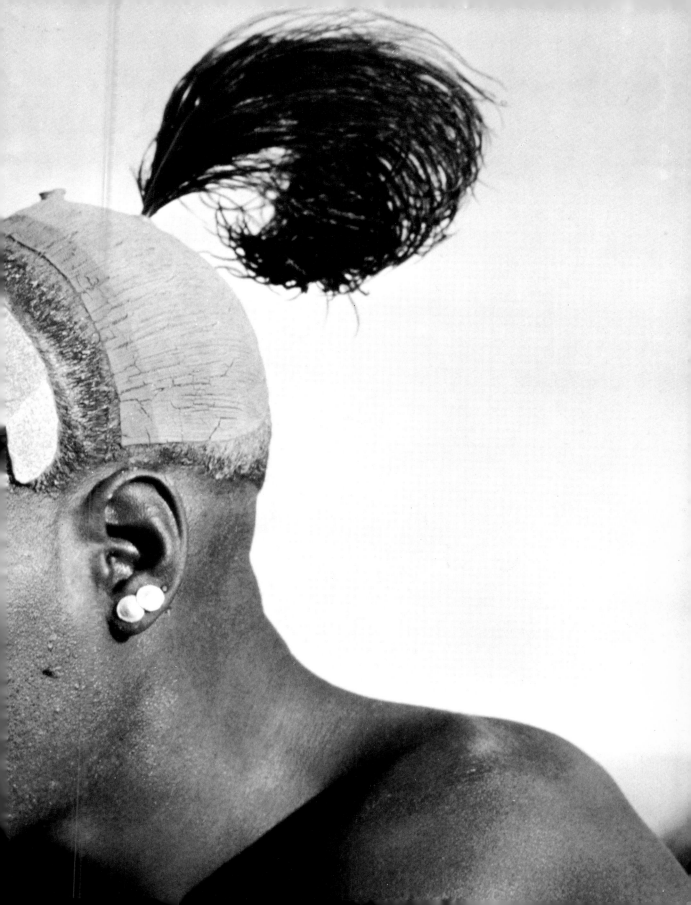

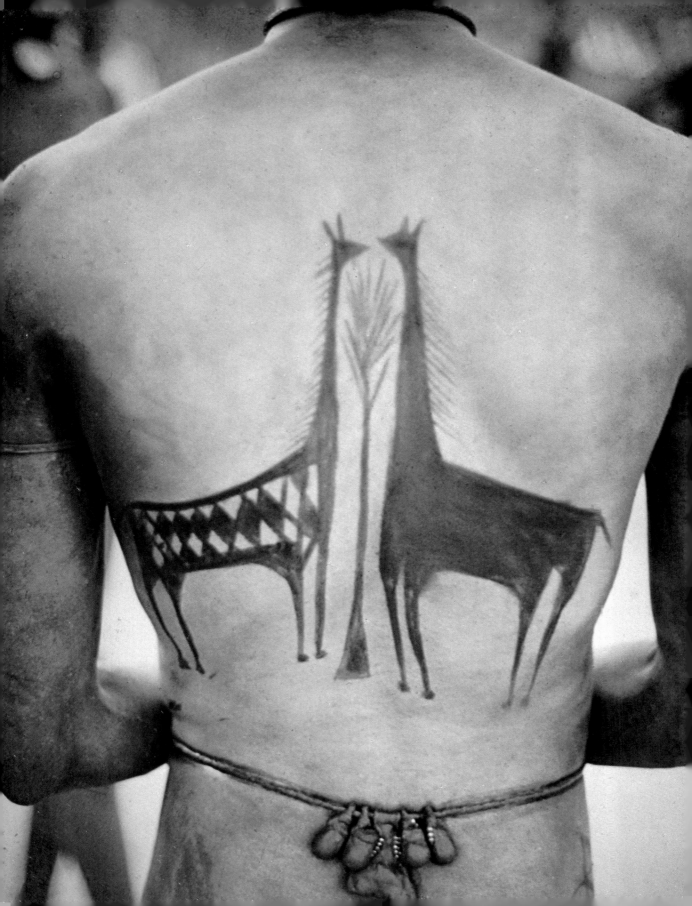

82. Many of the patterns used in Nuba body painting derive from the natural environment. The elegant shape of a giraffe lends itself admirably to this purpose.

distract attention from its form by any symbolic content. When a Nuba man paints a giraffe on his back he is not expressing a desire to take on the qualities of that animal; he wants only to complement his own form with the creature's elegant shape (plate 82). The decorated body is valued as an aesthetic object, and the designs which he applies are only a means to that end. Decoration can even remedy what are viewed as faults; eyes which are too small can be widened by circles of white clay, the natural contours of the face can be emphasized by dramatic lines drawn diagonally from the crown of the head towards the centre. Natural features become part of the design: the eye is the centre of a bird's wing, the hairline is integrated into a composite facial picture.

This concern with the body is evident in the Nuba vocabulary. They have words to refer to every muscle visible on the body, and even to the indentations between them; they can also refer by name to different styles of body movement and to the different sorts of walk, skip and prance executed by the warrior, and the significance they attach to the sheen and texture of the skin is also important to the Nuba. Faris notes that the Nuba make fine verbal distinctions between different sorts of abrasion to the skin, reflecting their great concern to preserve it from blemishes of any kind. Ideally, the skin should be gleaming with oil, burnished to a deep brown or black to represent health and well-being. Even if a man has been only slightly injured, resulting in a minor abrasion, he will not paint or call attention to his body in any way: dry, flaky skin is not merely considered unattractive, it signifies that a person has removed himself from normal social intercourse.

Tattoo

83. Despite interference from missionaries, some Maori women still retain a tattoo around their mouths; they believe it keeps them young and prevents the skin from shrivelling.

The tattoo, perhaps the most fascinating of all forms of body decoration, is found throughout the world, though it is less common among dark-skinned peoples. The word itself was introduced into the English language by Captain Cook on his return from the South Seas and comes from the Tahitian *tatu* 'to strike'; the Arabic *daqq* bears the same meaning, and both words refer to the technique of holding a sharp-pointed instrument against the skin and tapping it with a small mallet (plate 84).

In the Marquesas Islands the instrument, which was called a *ta*, was toothed and made of human bone. The artist used points of many different sizes to achieve the delicate fine lines and to fill in the solid patches of colour. Most *ta* were about three inches long and slightly wedge-shaped, with a series of small points like a comb to make the punctures; smaller curves in the design were made with the leg and wing bones of birds. The number of teeth varied up to about twenty; Herman Melville, who passed through the Marquesas Islands, reports the use of a *ta* with only one point as an example of the fine, painstaking quality of the work.

The traditional method among the Haida of the Northwest Coast was to use thorns, the spines of fish or pieces of bone to pierce the skin and then to rub the wound with pigment. Sometimes the piercing instrument was dipped first into the dye and then inserted under the skin. The colours most commonly observed were red, made from Chinese vermilion, and soot which gave a blue appearance under the skin. By the end of the nineteenth

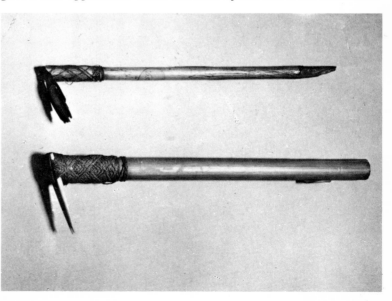

84. (*Right*) Instruments to pierce the skin were sometimes made from human or bird bones, and sometimes from thorns or pieces of carved wood: the point was held against the skin and tapped with a small mallet. Occasionally, the artist made notches in the handle to signify the number of people whom he had tattooed. Those shown are about 7 inches (17.5 cm) long.

century most Haida tattooing was done with European needles, which were said to be less painful and caused less bleeding than the cruder instruments of the past.

Among the Eskimos these marks were made with a needle and a thread which had been covered in soot; this was drawn underneath the skin, following a pattern and leaving a trail which formed into the appropriate design. The pigment most frequently used was charcoal or soot, which lent a bluish cast to the design. In the Marquesas Islands the pigment was prepared from the soot formed by the shells of a particular nut *(Aleurites triloba)* which had been placed over a fire; the soot was left on a stone to dry in the sun,

86. Engraving of an intricately tattooed Caduveo woman from Brazil. The asymmetrical design heightens the element of the mysterious in the tattoo pattern.

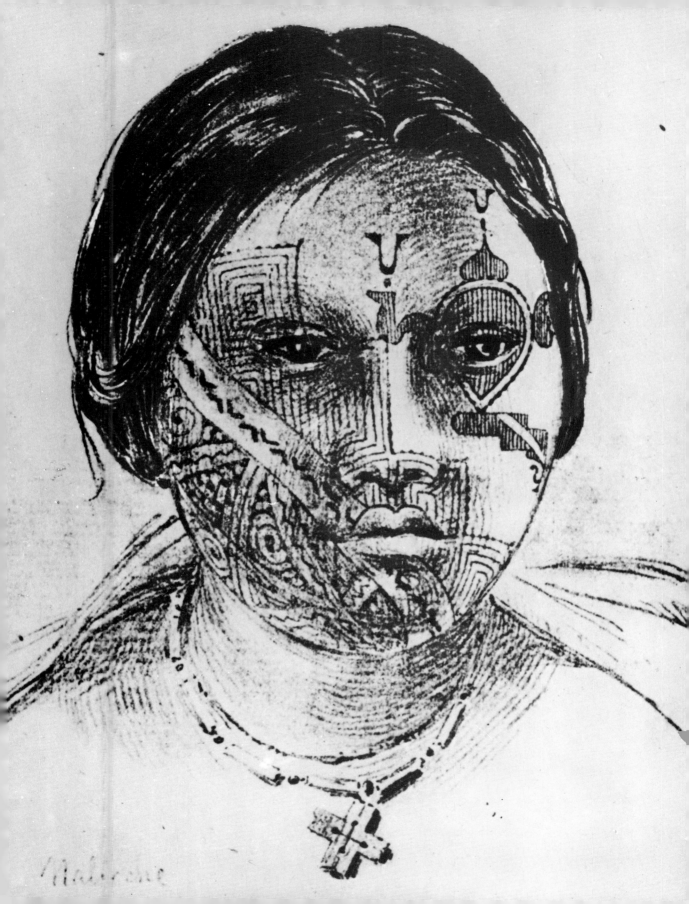

Malvane

and when the artist arrived, it was mixed either with coconut oil or plain water. The pigment itself sometimes enhanced the magical properties of the tattoo.

In Arab countries the tattoo is used both as an ornament and as a protection for the body by means of sympathetic magic (plate 87). The tattoo artists among the Arabs are usually women and the finest examples of their art are said to be achieved in Baghdad. Pigment for the tattoo sometimes had magical qualities; it could be prepared from the milk of a nursing mother — preferably from a woman nursing a daughter since the milk for a girl is said to be more soothing and cooler — and its strengthening properties, which help a child grow and flourish, would impart similar benefits to the wearer of the tattoo. Even greater protection was derived if a verse of the Koran was recited during the application of the tattoo.

Tattooing in the Marquesas Islands reached standards of artistry not seen elsewhere. A few men were recognized as masters and were in great demand, travelling about the islands with their instruments carried in a flat bamboo case. The artist first drew the design in charcoal and after he had outlined it in tattoo his assistants — usually four or five were on hand — were sometimes allowed to fill it in with cross-hatching or with solid

87. (*Above*) Bedouin women of Jordan believe that their tattoos make them more beautiful and that they keep away evil spirits.

88. Indian girl of Rajasthan. The three tattoo marks on her chin are a protection from evil.

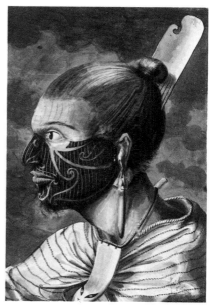

colour; they would thus acquire an expertise which would allow them to establish themselves as artists in their own right.

During the course of his work the artist would chant a song which was said to alleviate the pain. One such song is recorded by Melville in *Omoo*, a novel based on his travels in the South Seas:

> Where is that sound?
> In Hannamanoor.
> And wherefore that sound?
> The sound of a hundred hammers,
> Tapping, tapping, tapping
> The shark teeth.
>
> Where is that light?
> Round about the King's house.
> And the small laughter?
> The small, merry laughter, it is
> Of the sons and daughters of the tattooed.

The length of time spent with the artist varied depending on the patient's fortitude: the greater the stamina of his victim, the more quickly was the artist's job complete. The first sitting was spent outlining the major figures of the design on the breast, arms, back and thighs, and the design would be completed at intervals, spaced over three to six months. One man, according to tradition, was said to have been completely covered in three days; generally, however, the operation was performed only on one section of the body at a time and the patient then rested for three days. If fever ensued, sometimes with inflammation, the juice of banana leaves and an ointment from the hibiscus tree were used to treat the afflictions.

The tattoo was not only an artistic achievement: it also demonstrated that its recipient could bear pain. On one island, the

89. *(Above left)* A Marquesan mother receives her tattoos. The tattooing of Marquesan men involved ritual sanctions and a period of seclusion; women were tattooed in their own home and with comparatively little ceremony.

90. *(Above)* Portrait of a Maori, painted on one of Cook's voyages in the 1770s. The tattoo is characterized by its symmetry: the design divides in half along the bridge of the nose, and each side of the face is marked with spirals, curves and whorls. Similar patterns occur on Maori door-posts, roof-beams and canoes.

91. Rauperaha, leader of the Maori rebellion which culminated with the Wairau massacre in 1867. Maori facial tattoos were so distinctive and varied so widely that chiefs would draw them at the foot of European treaties in place of their signatures.

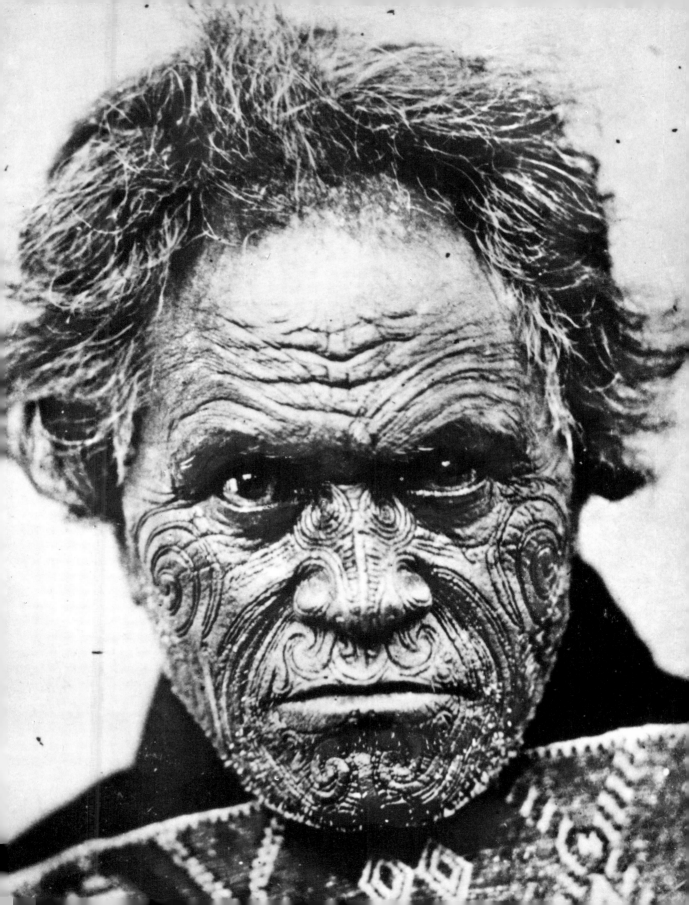

92. (*Left*) Portrait of a Marquesan prince by F. Savage. Note how the design emphasizes the body's natural contours.

word to describe a person who was completely covered with tattoos is *ne'one'o*, based on a word meaning either 'to cry for a long time' or 'horrific'. One observer in the Marquesas noted that whenever people discussed the tattoo design, they emphasized the pain with which it was acquired.

For Marquesas women there were no elaborate rites surrounding the tattooing as there were for the men. They were tattooed only on their arms and hands, the abdomen and the lower back, while the full tattoo for a man covered his entire body except for the genitals, extending over the crown of the head, inside the mouth and nose and on the eyelids. The islanders displayed their art on the body as a whole (in contrast to the Maori, who concentrated chiefly on the face), reserving the most elaborate decoration for the exposed parts of the body. Parts of the body covered by clothes often received only a rudimentary pattern, but this emphasis changed when the French prohibited the practice in 1884; although the islanders continued surreptitiously to tattoo they were forced to apply their designs only to parts of their bodies hidden by their clothing.

The tattooing of the islanders displayed the flowing grace of a body in action (plate 92). The circular motif tattooed underneath a warrior's arm showed off to advantage when he raised his arm to

93. Among the Iban of Sarawak the tattoo was once a sign of military valour. It was made by impressing the skin with a wooden block in which sharp points had been arranged to form the desired pattern; today, European needles are used and the tattoo has become ornamental.

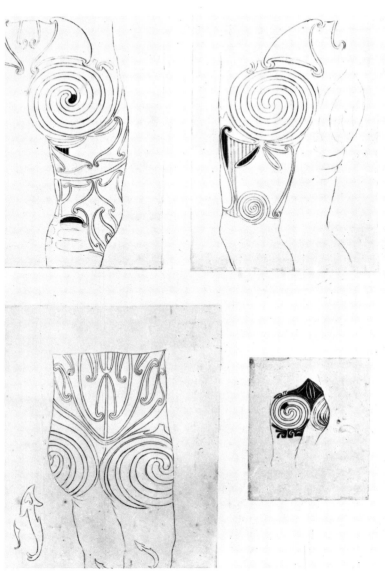

94. *(Left)* Sketches of Maori body designs observed during the 1770s. The double spiral was unique to the Maori; single spirals are common throughout the South Seas.

strike with his war club, and the women's hands and fingers were tattooed with swirling, spiralling shapes which flashed up and down as they prepared their food; joints were highlighted with a series of triangles and circles which emphasized the dynamic quality of the design. Thick horizontal bands across the face gave an impression of hoops encircling the head, front and back, though in fact they covered only the front, stopping at the ears. The designs on the shoulder and chest emphasized the forceful stance of the men as they stood with their arms crossed behind their backs, and the insides of their knees were marked elaborately because they were visible when the men sat cross-legged.

Over the centuries the Marquesas designs seem to have fluctuated according to social changes, just as any fashion does, and to have varied from island to island. In 1595 the Spanish explorer Mendaña

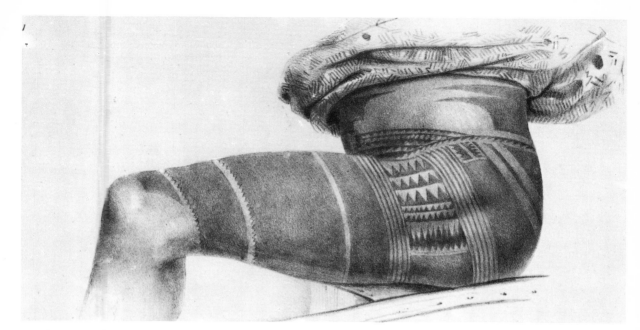

95. Thick solid patches, with a toothed border and a flame-like pattern, distinguish this thigh tattoo as coming from Nuka Hiva one of the Marquesas Islands. Such heavily marked flesh was a sign that the individual had endured great pain.

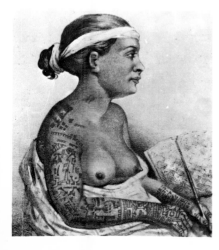

96. Portrait of a seated Marquesan woman with plaited fan. A more common design for the arms and on the shoulders showed abstract representations of plants, shellfish and other animals.

described the fish and birds painted upon the body, the men sporting lizards on their faces and the women with patterns of birds and fish behind their ears. By 1772, according to J. R. Forster, the decoration had changed to geometric patterns — 'blotches, spirals, bars, chequers and lines'. In the early twentieth century old people still displayed these patterns, with the addition of rounded forms, circles and half-circles. Naturalistic representations, although highly stylized, were common — the most usual were fish, seaweed, birds and shells (plate 96); after the first European presence, one ingenious tattooer devised a pattern for the legs based on a pair of boots.

Each design had a specific name — 'a row of evil spirits', or 'the sacred bathing place of the chiefs' — and could be requested by the customer accordingly. The geometric patterns varied according to the part of the body and certain patterns were deemed appropriate to particular limbs: legs, for example, were often covered with triangular patches, arranged to form a central line interspersed with curving tendrils. On other parts of the body large rectangular patches were coloured in with heavy dark lines surrounded by fanciful designs — oak leaves, perhaps, or fretted motifs with flame-like edges (plate 95).

Such designs are as remarkable for the immediacy of their visual impact as for their enduring quality. They represent a force that seems to subsume the distinctive features of the individual, taking on a life of their own. In a striking comparison of Maori tattoo and Caduveo face painting Lévi-Strauss notes that in each case the facial features are ignored in the creation of the design: 'the design is the face, or rather it creates it. It is the design which confers upon the face its social existence, its human dignity, its spiritual significance.'

Bibliography

General theory of anthropology

Leach, Edmund: *Ritualization in Man*. Philosophical Transactions of the Royal Society, vol. 251, 1966

Lévi-Strauss, Claude: *Structural Anthropology*. New York, Basic Books, 1963

General ethnography

Deacon, A. Bernard: *Malekula: A Vanishing People in the New Hebrides*. London, George Routledge and Sons, 1934

Hilger, Inez M: *Together with the Ainu: A Vanishing People*. Norman, Oklahoma, Oklahoma University Press, 1971

Specific accounts of body decoration

Faris, James: *Nuba Personal Art*. London, Gerald Duckworth and Co., 1972

Ganay, Solange de: *On a form of Cicatrisation among the Bambara*. Man, vol. XLIX, no. 65, pages 53–55

Handy, Willowdean: *Tattooing in the Marquesas*. Bulletin of the Bernice P. Bishop Museum, 1922

Mallery, Garrick: *Picture Writing of the American Indians*. New York, Dover Publications Inc., 1972

Phillipps, W. J: *An Introduction to the Study of Tattooing Chisels of the Maori with Notes on Tattoo*. Dominion Records in Ethnology, vol. 1, no 3, 1948

Smeaton, Winifred: *Tattooing among the Arabs of Iraq*. American Anthropologist, vol. 39, 1937

Strathern, Andrew and Marilyn: *Self-Decoration in Mount Hagen*. London, Gerald Duckworth and Co., 1971

Turner, Terence: *Tchikrin, A Central Brazilian Tribe and its Symbolic Language of Bodily Adornment*. Natural History, vol. 78, 1969

Turner, Victor: *Three Symbols of Passage in Neembu Circumcision Ritual*, in Essays on Rituals of Social Relations, ed. Max Gluckman. Manchester, Manchester University Press, 1962

Acknowledgements and list of illustrations

The author and Blacker Calmann Cooper Ltd would like to thank the photographers and photographic agencies who allowed their photographs to be reproduced in this book. They would also like to thank the museums and libraries who allowed works from their collections to be reproduced.

Cover Subject: Txicão Indian. Photo Claus C. Meyer (Black Star)
1. Chief at the Mount Hagen show, New Guinea. Photo D. Frobisch (Zefa)
2. Aiome man of New Guinea. Photo Haddon Coll., Cambridge
3. Masai youth. Photo Black Star
4. Man of New Guinea with scarab beetle horns in his nose. Photo M. Folco (Black Star)
5. Two Polynesian women with scarification. Photo Haddon Coll., Cambridge
6. Sandwich Islands chief. British Museum, London
7. Chin woman with choker. Photo Haddon Coll., Cambridge
8. Bakoba bride from Transvaal with choker. Photo Liedmann (Zefa)
9. Wai-Wai boy. Photo Nicholas Guppy
10. Lip-plugs from the Northwest Coast of America. British Museum, London
11. Chad woman with lip-plug. Photo J. Bitsch (Zefa)
12. Hamar man of southern Ethiopia. Photo Strecker
13. Fulani woman of Niger. Photo V. Engelbert (Zefa)
14. Ghanaian shaman. Photo E. Ikonomou
15. Ivory coast shaman. Photo E. Ikonomou
16. Tattooed woman of the Sandwich Islands. British Museum, London
17. Polynesian men. British Museum, London
18. Sioux Indian chief, drawing from *Codex Canadiensis*. Thomas Gilcrease Institute, Tulsa
19. Marquesas Islander, painted by H. Ainsworth. National Library of Australia (Rex Nan Kivell Coll.), Canberra
20. Cameroon woman with scarification. Photo V. Engelbert (Zefa)
21. Maori princess with tattoo. Photo John Hillelson Agency
22. Young African with scars. Photo Haddon Coll., Cambridge
23. Ghanaian woman with facial scars. Photo E. Ikonomou
24. Yemeni hand patterns. Photo S. Kennedy
25. Yemeni hand patterns. Photo S. Kennedy
26. Yemeni feet painting. Photo S. Kennedy
27. Australian aborigine with roll scars. Photo Haddon Coll., Cambridge
28. Australian aborigine youths with scars. Photo Haddon Coll., Cambridge
29. Australian aborigine having a tooth knocked out. Photo Axel Poignant
30. Boy from Central Africa with filed teeth. Photo Haddon Coll., Cambridge
31. Bali wall plaque showing monster with sharpened teeth. Photo Peter Ramsden
32–35. Sequence showing the scarification of a baby from Gonja tribe in northern Ghana. Photo E. Ikonomou
36. Chinook Indian mother and child, painted by Paul Kane. Museum of Fine Arts, Montreal
37. Man from Malekula, New Hebrides, with flattened head. Photo Haddon Coll., Cambridge
38. Bopoto mother and child. Photo Haddon Coll., Cambridge
39. Amazonian Indians with body painting. Photo Claus C. Meyer (Black Star)
40. Australian aborigines with body painting. Photo Axel Poignant
41. Youths from New Britain with body painting. Photo Haddon Coll., Cambridge
42. Masai youths with scars. Photo Black Star
43. Panare boys, south Venezuela. Photo Pau Henley
44. Girl from southwestern Ghana being decorated prior to her marriage. Photo E. Ikonomou
45. Girl from southwestern Ghana being painted prior to her marriage. Photo E. Ikonomou
46. Australian aborigine initiation rites. Photo Axel Poignant
47. Bopoto woman with scars. Photo Haddon Coll., Cambridge
48. Nuba men with partially shaved heads and painted faces. Photo G. Rodger (John Hillelson Agency)
49. Yemeni infant with painted face. Photo N. Mundy
50. Suiá man with lip-plug. Photo E. Schultes (Black Star)
51. Nineteenth-century print of Caroline Islanders. British Museum, London
52. Nuba girl with scars. Photo O. Luz (Zefa)
53. Nuba girl with scars. Photo J. Faris
54. Indian from North American plains. Photo Royal Geographical Society
55. Bopoto initiation rite involving scarification. Photo Haddon Coll., Cambridge
56. Eastern Timacuan Indian, painted by John White. British Museum, London
57. Australian aborigine from Aurunkun, Cape York Peninsula, being painted. Photo E. Cranstone (Axel Poignant)

Index